HOMEMADE DOG TREATS USING BAKING MATS

Dr. Wesley Glasgow

DISCLAIMER

The content within this book reflects my thoughts, experiences, and beliefs. It is meant for informational and entertainment purposes. While I have taken great care to provide accurate information, I cannot guarantee the absolute correctness or applicability of the content to every individual or situation. Please consult with relevant professionals for advice specific to your needs.

TABLE OF CONTENTS

INTRODUCTION

In the soft embrace of dawn's gentle light, amidst the whispers of a childhood filled with wonder and furry companionship, my journey began. A journey that would weave its way through the tapestry of time, touching the hearts of those who share in the boundless love of our faithful four-legged friends.

Growing up, I was enveloped in a world where wagging tails and wet noses were the melodies that serenaded my soul. It was a world where each bark echoed with the promise of unwavering loyalty and unconditional love. And in the midst of it all stood Dan, my first canine companion, a beacon of joy in the labyrinth of life.

Dan was not just a dog; he was a cherished member of our family, a guardian of our hearts. From the moment he entered our lives, he became my steadfast companion, my confidant, my closest friend. Together, we embarked on countless adventures, weaving tales of laughter and love beneath the azure canopy of the sky.

But as the years unfurled their tapestry, I began to notice subtle changes in Dan's demeanor. His once boundless energy began to wane, his playful spirit dimming like a flickering flame in the twilight. And yet, despite my fervent efforts to shower him with love and affection, I failed to see the silent cries of his body, the whispers of pain hidden beneath his stoic facade.

It was not until that fateful day, when the shadows of illness cast their somber veil over our home, that I realized the gravity of my oversight. Dan, my beloved companion, was battling a silent adversary, a foe that lurked within the shadows of his own body. Diabetes had stolen into his life like a thief in the night, robbing him of his vitality and robbing me of my innocence.

As I stood by his side, watching the flicker of life dance in his weary eyes, I knew that something had to change. I could no longer stand idly by as the sands of time slipped through my fingers like grains of sand in the wind. With a heart heavy with regret and a resolve forged in the fires of love, I vowed to embark on a journey of discovery, a quest to unlock the secrets of health and vitality for our beloved companions.

And so, with Dan as my guiding light, I delved into the realm of nutrition, seeking solace in the pages of ancient wisdom and the wisdom of modern science. I immersed myself in the alchemy of culinary arts, blending ingredients with the precision of a master craftsman, crafting recipes that would nourish not only the body but also the soul.

Through years of dedication and tireless exploration, I honed my skills, transforming my passion into a vocation, my love into a legacy. Today, as a veterinarian and seasoned cook, I stand as a beacon of hope in a world shrouded in uncertainty, a voice of compassion in a sea of indifference.

But my journey is far from over, for the path that lies before me is fraught with challenges and opportunities, trials and triumphs. And yet, as I gaze upon the horizon, I am filled with a sense of purpose, a conviction that my mission is far greater than the sum of its parts.

For within the pages of this humble cookbook, you will find not just recipes, but a roadmap to a world of health and happiness for your beloved companions. You will discover the transformative power of good nutrition, the healing touch of a loving heart, and the boundless joy that comes from sharing a meal with those we hold dear.

So let us embark on this journey together, hand in paw, as we explore the wondrous tapestry of flavors and aromas that await us. Let us celebrate the beauty of life and the gift of friendship, as we nourish our bodies and souls with each delectable bite.

For in the end, it is not the destination that defines us, but the journey we take and the lives we touch along the way. And as we tread the path of life's great adventure, , may we always remember the profound truth that love knows no bounds, and that in the hearts of our faithful companions, we find the truest reflection of our own humanity.

Welcome, dear reader, to a world of culinary delights and canine companionship. Welcome to the journey of a lifetime.

Contact the Author

Thank you for reading my book! I would love to hear from you, whether you have feedback, questions, or just want to share your thoughts. Your feedback means a lot to me and helps me improve as a writer.

Please don't hesitate to reach out to me through

glasgowesley@gmail.com

I look forward to connecting with my readers and appreciate your support in this literary journey. Your thoughts and comments are valuable to me.

Chapter 1
Baking Basics

Baking mats are essential tools for any baker, offering numerous benefits that contribute to better baking outcomes. Understanding how to use them safely and effectively can elevate your baking game. Additionally, exploring alternative baking surface options provides flexibility and versatility in your baking endeavours.

Understanding Baking Mats and Their Benefits

Baking mats, also known as silicone baking mats or silicone baking sheets, are thin, flexible sheets made from food-grade silicone. They serve as non-stick surfaces for baking, replacing the need for parchment paper or greasing baking pans. Here are some key benefits of using baking mats:

1. **Non-stick Properties**: Baking mats provide a non-stick surface, preventing baked goods from sticking to the pan and ensuring easy release.

2. **Even Heat Distribution**: The silicone material distributes heat evenly, promoting consistent baking results across the entire surface of your baked goods.

3. **Reusable and Eco-Friendly**: Baking mats are reusable, reducing the need for disposable parchment paper and promoting sustainability in baking practices.

4. **Easy Cleanup**: Baking mats are dishwasher safe and easy to clean by hand, saving time and effort in post-baking cleanup.

5. **Versatility**: Baking mats can withstand a wide range of temperatures, making them suitable for various baking tasks, including cookies, pastries, and even roasting vegetables.

Tips for Using Baking Mats Safely and Effectively

To maximize the benefits of baking mats and ensure safe usage, consider the following tips:

1. **Proper Placement**: Always place the baking mat on a sturdy baking sheet or pan before adding your batter or dough. Avoid using baking mats directly on oven racks, as they may not provide sufficient support.

2. **Avoid Sharp Objects**: Refrain from cutting or slicing food directly on the baking mat, as sharp utensils can damage the silicone surface. Instead, transfer baked goods to a cutting board before slicing.

3. **Monitor Temperature**: While baking mats are heat-resistant, it's essential to adhere to recommended temperature limits specified by the manufacturer to prevent damage.

4. **Avoid Abrasive Cleaners**: Use mild dish soap and a soft sponge or cloth to clean baking mats. Avoid abrasive cleaners or scrubbers that can scratch the surface and compromise its non-stick properties.

5. **Store Properly**: Roll or stack baking mats neatly to prevent creases or folds that may affect their performance. Store them in a cool, dry place away from direct sunlight.

Alternative Baking Surface Options

While baking mats offer convenience and versatility, several alternative baking surface options can be used depending on your preferences and specific baking needs:

1. **Parchment Paper**: Parchment paper is a traditional option for lining baking pans, offering easy release and minimal cleanup. It's disposable, making it ideal for certain baking tasks.

2. **Silicone Baking Pans**: Silicone baking pans are molded from silicone material, eliminating the need for additional liners. They offer non-stick properties similar to baking mats and are reusable.

3. **Aluminum Foil**: Aluminum foil can be used as a makeshift liner for baking pans, although it may not provide the same non-stick benefits as silicone mats or parchment paper. It's best suited for roasting or wrapping foods.

4. **Greased Baking Pans**: Greasing baking pans with butter, oil, or cooking spray is a traditional method for preventing sticking. While effective, it may result in uneven browning and require additional cleanup.

By understanding the benefits of baking mats, following safety guidelines, and exploring alternative baking surface options, you can enhance your baking experience and achieve delicious results with ease.

Chapter 2
Nutritious Ingredients

Selecting the right ingredients for your dog's treats is crucial for their overall health and well-being. By understanding which ingredients to include and which ones to avoid, as well as the benefits of incorporating superfoods, you can ensure that your furry friend enjoys delicious and nutritious homemade treats.

Choosing the Best Ingredients for Your Dog's Health

When making treats for your dog, opt for ingredients that provide essential nutrients while being gentle on their digestive system. Here are some nutritious ingredients to consider:

1. **Lean Proteins**: Choose high-quality, lean proteins such as chicken, turkey, beef, or fish. Proteins are vital for muscle development and overall health.

2. **Whole Grains**: Incorporate whole grains like oats, brown rice, or quinoa for complex carbohydrates that provide sustained energy and fiber for digestive health.

3. **Fruits and Vegetables**: Include dog-friendly fruits and vegetables such as apples, carrots, blueberries, and sweet potatoes. These ingredients are rich in vitamins, minerals, and antioxidants.

4. **Healthy Fats**: Use sources of healthy fats like coconut oil, olive oil, or salmon oil to support your dog's skin and coat health, as well as their immune system.

5. **Natural Sweeteners**: When adding sweetness to treats, opt for natural alternatives like honey or mashed banana in moderation.

Common Ingredients to Avoid in Dog Treats

Certain ingredients can be harmful to dogs and should be avoided when making homemade treats. These include:

1. **Artificial Sweeteners**: Avoid artificial sweeteners such as xylitol, which can be toxic to dogs and lead to severe health issues like liver damage and hypoglycemia.

2. **Chocolate**: Chocolate contains theobromine, a compound that is toxic to dogs and can cause vomiting, diarrhea, tremors, and even death in severe cases.

3. **Grapes and Raisins**: Grapes and raisins can cause kidney failure in dogs, so it's essential to steer clear of these ingredients in homemade treats.

4. **Onions and Garlic**: Onions and garlic, whether raw, cooked, or powdered, contain compounds that can damage a dog's red blood cells and lead to anemia.

5. **High-Fat Foods**: Avoid using excessive amounts of fatty ingredients like butter or bacon, as they can contribute to obesity and pancreatitis in dogs.

The Role of Superfoods in Homemade Treats

Incorporating superfoods into your dog's treats can provide an extra nutritional boost. Superfoods are nutrient-dense ingredients that offer various health benefits. Some superfoods suitable for dogs include:

1. **Pumpkin**: Rich in fiber and vitamins, pumpkin can aid in digestion and regulate bowel movements in dogs.

2. **Spinach**: Spinach is packed with vitamins A, C, and K, as well as iron and antioxidants, making it a nutritious addition to homemade treats.

3. **Coconut**: Coconut contains medium-chain fatty acids, which can improve your dog's skin and coat health and support their immune system.

4. **Chia Seeds**: Chia seeds are an excellent source of omega-3 fatty acids, fiber, and protein, promoting heart health and aiding digestion in dogs.

5. **Turmeric**: Turmeric possesses anti-inflammatory properties and can help alleviate joint pain and arthritis symptoms in dogs.

OTHER BOOKS BY THE AUTHOR

INSTANT POT DOG FOOD COOKBOOK

DOG FOOD COOKBOOK FOR PICKY EATERS

AIR FRYER DOG FOOD COOKBOOK

SLOW COOKER DOG FOOD COOKBOOK

DOG FOOD COOKBOOK FOR SENSITIVE STOMACH

SCAN THE QR CODE TO SEE MORE BOOKS BY AUTHOR

Chapter 3
Dog Treats

Peanut Butter Banana Bites

Cooking Time: 10-12 minutes

Servings: Makes about 12 treats

Ingredients:

- 1 ripe banana, mashed

- 1/2 cup natural peanut butter

- 1 cup oats

Instructions:

1. Preheat your oven to 350°F (175°C) and line a baking sheet with a silicone baking mat.

2. In a mixing bowl, combine mashed banana, peanut butter, and oats until well combined.

3. Roll the mixture into small balls and place them on the prepared baking mat.

4. Flatten each ball with a fork to create a cookie shape.

5. Bake for 10-12 minutes until lightly golden brown.

6. Allow to cool completely before serving.

Nutritional Information: Each treat provides approximately 60 calories, 2g protein, 3g fat, 8g carbohydrates, 1g Fiber

Blueberry Oatmeal Squares

Cooking Time: 15-20 minutes

Servings: Makes about 16 squares

Ingredients:

- 1 cup blueberries

- 1 cup oats

- 1/4 cup unsweetened applesauce

- 1/4 cup water

Instructions:

1. Preheat your oven to 350°F (175°C) and line a baking sheet with a silicone baking mat.

2. In a blender or food processor, blend blueberries, oats, applesauce, and water until smooth.

3. Spread the mixture evenly onto the prepared baking mat.

4. Bake for 15-20 minutes until firm and lightly golden.

5. Allow to cool, then cut into squares using a knife or pizza cutter.

6. Store in an airtight container.

Nutritional Information: Each square provides approximately 40 calories, 1g protein, 0.5g fat, 9g carbohydrates, 1g Fiber

Carrot and Apple Dog Biscuits

Cooking Time: 20-25 minutes

Servings: Makes about 20 biscuits

Ingredients:

- 1 cup grated carrot

- 1 cup grated apple

- 1 1/2 cups whole wheat flour

- 1 egg

Instructions:

1. Preheat your oven to 350°F (175°C) and line a baking sheet with a silicone baking mat.

2. In a large bowl, combine grated carrot, grated apple, whole wheat flour, and egg until a dough forms.

3. Roll out the dough on a floured surface to about 1/4-inch thickness.

4. Use cookie cutters to cut out shapes and place them on the prepared baking mat.

5. Bake for 20-25 minutes until biscuits are golden brown and firm.

6. Allow to cool completely before storing in an airtight container.

Nutritional Information: Each biscuit provides approximately 45 calories, 1g protein, 0.5g fat, 9g carbohydrates, 1g Fiber

Sweet Potato and Peanut Butter Bones

Cooking Time: 30-35 minutes

Servings: Makes about 15 bones

Ingredients:

- 1 cup cooked and mashed sweet potato

- 1/4 cup natural peanut butter

- 1 1/2 cups oat flour

- 1 egg

Instructions:

1. Preheat your oven to 350°F (175°C) and line a baking sheet with a silicone baking mat.

2. In a mixing bowl, combine mashed sweet potato, peanut butter, oat flour, and egg until well combined.

3. Roll out the dough on a floured surface to about 1/4-inch thickness.

4. Use bone-shaped cookie cutters to cut out shapes and place them on the prepared baking mat.

5. Bake for 30-35 minutes until bones are firm and slightly browned.

6. Allow to cool completely before serving.

Nutritional Information: Each bone provides approximately 65 calories, 2g protein, 3g fat, 8g carbohydrates, 1g Fiber

Pumpkin and Cinnamon Dog Cookies

Cooking Time: 15-18 minutes

Servings: Makes about 24 cookies

Ingredients:

- 1 cup canned pumpkin puree

- 2 cups whole wheat flour

- 1 teaspoon ground cinnamon

- 1 egg

Instructions:

1. Preheat your oven to 350°F (175°C) and line a baking sheet with a silicone baking mat.

2. In a mixing bowl, combine pumpkin puree, whole wheat flour, ground cinnamon, and egg until a dough forms.

3. Roll out the dough on a floured surface to about 1/4-inch thickness.

4. Use cookie cutters to cut out shapes and place them on the prepared baking mat.

5. Bake for 15-18 minutes until cookies are firm and lightly browned.

6. Allow to cool completely before storing in an airtight container.

Nutritional Information: Each cookie provides approximately 35 calories, 1g protein, 0.5g fat, 7g carbohydrates, 1g Fiber

Chicken and Cheese Treats

Cooking Time: 10-12 minutes

Servings: Makes about 20 treats

Ingredients:

- 1 cup cooked and shredded chicken

- 1/2 cup shredded cheese (cheddar or mozzarella)

- 1 cup oat flour

- 1 egg

Instructions:

1. Preheat your oven to 350°F (175°C) and line a baking sheet with a silicone baking mat.

2. In a mixing bowl, combine shredded chicken, shredded cheese, oat flour, and egg until well combined.

3. Roll the mixture into small balls and place them on the prepared baking mat.

4. Flatten each ball slightly with your fingers or a fork.

5. Bake for 10-12 minutes until treats are cooked through and lightly golden.

6. Allow to cool completely before serving.

Nutritional Information: Each treat provides approximately 45 calories, 3g protein, 2g fat, 4g carbohydrates, 1g Fiber

Turkey and Cranberry Biscuits

Cooking Time: 25-30 minutes

Servings: Makes about 15 biscuits

Ingredients:

- 1 cup cooked and shredded turkey

- 1/4 cup dried cranberries, chopped

- 1 1/2 cups brown rice flour

- 1 egg

Instructions:

1. Preheat your oven to 350°F (175°C) and line a baking sheet with a silicone baking mat.

2. In a mixing bowl, combine shredded turkey, chopped dried cranberries, brown rice flour, and egg until a dough forms.

3. Roll out the dough on a floured surface to about 1/4-inch thickness.

4. Use cookie cutters to cut out shapes and place them on the prepared baking mat.

5. Bake for 25-30 minutes until biscuits are firm and lightly browned.

6. Allow to cool completely before storing in an airtight container.

Nutritional Information: Each biscuit provides approximately 55 calories, 3g protein, 1g fat, 9g carbohydrates, 1g Fiber

Salmon and Sweet Potato Bars

Cooking Time: 30-35 minutes

Servings: Makes about 12 bars

Ingredients:

- 1 cup cooked and mashed sweet potato

- 1 can (6 ounces) salmon, drained and flaked

- 1 1/2 cups oat flour

- 1 egg

Instructions:

1. Preheat your oven to 350°F (175°C) and line a baking sheet with a silicone baking mat.

2. In a mixing bowl, combine mashed sweet potato, flaked salmon, oat flour, and egg until well combined.

3. Spread the mixture evenly onto the prepared baking mat.

4. Bake for 30-35 minutes until bars are firm and lightly browned on the edges.

5. Allow to cool, then cut into bars using a knife or pizza cutter.

6. Store in an airtight container.

Nutritional Information: Each bar provides approximately 70 calories, 4g protein, 2g fat, 10g carbohydrates, 1g Fiber

Spinach and Cheese Balls

Cooking Time: 12-15 minutes

Servings: Makes about 18 balls

Ingredients:

- 1 cup chopped spinach, cooked and drained

- 1/2 cup shredded cheese (cheddar or mozzarella)

- 1 cup oat flour

- 1 egg

Instructions:

1. Preheat your oven to 350°F (175°C) and line a baking sheet with a silicone baking mat.

2. In a mixing bowl, combine chopped cooked spinach, shredded cheese, oat flour, and egg until well combined.

3. Roll the mixture into small balls and place them on the prepared baking mat.

4. Flatten each ball slightly with your fingers.

5. Bake for 12-15 minutes until treats are cooked through and lightly golden.

6. Allow to cool completely before serving.

Nutritional Information: Each ball provides approximately 40 calories, 2g protein, 1.5g fat, 5g carbohydrates, 1g Fiber

Beef and Carrot Sticks

Cooking Time: 18-20 minutes

Servings: Makes about 16 sticks

Ingredients:

- 1 cup cooked and shredded beef

- 1/2 cup grated carrot

- 1 1/2 cups whole wheat flour

- 1 egg

Instructions:

1. Preheat your oven to 350°F (175°C) and line a baking sheet with a silicone baking mat.

2. In a mixing bowl, combine shredded beef, grated carrot, whole wheat flour, and egg until a dough forms.

3. Roll out the dough on a floured surface into long sticks.

4. Place the sticks on the prepared baking mat.

5. Bake for 18-20 minutes until sticks are firm and lightly browned.

6. Allow to cool completely before storing in an airtight container.

Nutritional Information: Each stick provides approximately 50 calories, 3g protein, 1g fat, 8g carbohydrates, 1g Fiber

Chapter 4

Dog Biscuits and Chew

Pumpkin and Peanut Butter Biscuits

Cooking Time: 20-25 minutes

Servings: Makes about 20 biscuits

Ingredients:

- 1 cup canned pumpkin puree

- 1/4 cup natural peanut butter

- 2 1/2 cups whole wheat flour

- 1 egg

Instructions:

1. Preheat your oven to 350°F (175°C) and line a baking sheet with a silicone baking mat.

2. In a large bowl, mix together pumpkin puree, peanut butter, whole wheat flour, and egg until a dough forms.

3. Roll out the dough on a floured surface to about 1/4-inch thickness.

4. Use cookie cutters to cut out shapes and place them on the prepared baking mat.

5. Bake for 20-25 minutes until biscuits are firm and lightly browned.

6. Allow to cool completely before serving.

Nutritional Information: Each biscuit provides approximately 60 calories, 2g protein, 3g fat, 7g carbohydrates, 1g Fiber

Sweet Potato Chews

Cooking Time: 2 hours

Servings: Makes about 12 chews

Ingredients:

- 2 large sweet potatoes

Instructions:

1. Preheat your oven to 250°F (120°C) and line a baking sheet with a silicone baking mat.

2. Wash and scrub the sweet potatoes thoroughly.

3. Cut the sweet potatoes into thin slices, about 1/4-inch thick.

4. Place the slices on the prepared baking mat in a single layer.

5. Bake for 2 hours, flipping halfway through, until the chews are dried and slightly crispy.

6. Allow to cool completely before serving.

Nutritional Information: Each chew provides approximately 30 calories, 1g protein, 0g fat, 7g carbohydrates, 1g Fiber

Carrot and Apple Biscuits

Cooking Time: 25-30 minutes

Servings: Makes about 24 biscuits

Ingredients:

- 1 cup grated carrot

- 1 cup grated apple

- 2 cups oat flour

- 1 egg

Instructions:

1. Preheat your oven to 350°F (175°C) and line a baking sheet with a silicone baking mat.

2. In a mixing bowl, combine grated carrot, grated apple, oat flour, and egg until well combined.

3. Roll out the dough on a floured surface to about 1/4-inch thickness.

4. Use cookie cutters to cut out shapes and place them on the prepared baking mat.

5. Bake for 25-30 minutes until biscuits are firm and lightly browned.

6. Allow to cool completely before serving.

Nutritional Information: Each biscuit provides approximately 50 calories, 1.5g protein, 1g fat, 9g carbohydrates, 1g Fiber

Chicken Jerky

Cooking Time: 2-3 hours

Servings: Makes about 12 strips

Ingredients:

- 2 boneless, skinless chicken breasts

Instructions:

1. Preheat your oven to 200°F (95°C) and line a baking sheet with a silicone baking mat.

2. Slice the chicken breasts into thin strips, about 1/4-inch wide.

3. Place the strips on the prepared baking mat in a single layer.

4. Bake for 2-3 hours until the chicken is dried and jerky-like.

5. Allow to cool completely before serving.

Nutritional Information: Each strip provides approximately 25 calories, 5g protein, 0g fat, 0g carbohydrates, 0g Fiber

Banana and Blueberry Biscuits

Cooking Time: 20-25 minutes

Servings: Makes about 18 biscuits

Ingredients:

- 1 ripe banana, mashed

- 1/2 cup blueberries, mashed

- 2 cups oat flour

- 1 egg

Instructions:

1. Preheat your oven to 350°F (175°C) and line a baking sheet with a silicone baking mat.

2. In a mixing bowl, combine mashed banana, mashed blueberries, oat flour, and egg until well combined.

3. Roll out the dough on a floured surface to about 1/4-inch thickness.

4. Use cookie cutters to cut out shapes and place them on the prepared baking mat.

5. Bake for 20-25 minutes until biscuits are firm and lightly browned.

6. Allow to cool completely before serving.

Nutritional Information: Each biscuit provides approximately 45 calories, 1.5g protein, 1g fat, 8g carbohydrates, 1g Fiber

Peanut Butter and Bacon Biscuits

Cooking Time: 25-30 minutes

Servings: Makes about 16 biscuits

Ingredients:

- 1/2 cup natural peanut butter

- 1/4 cup cooked and crumbled bacon

- 2 cups whole wheat flour

- 1 egg

Instructions:

1. Preheat your oven to 350°F (175°C) and line a baking sheet with a silicone baking mat.

2. In a mixing bowl, combine peanut butter, crumbled bacon, whole wheat flour, and egg until a dough forms.

3. Roll out the dough on a floured surface to about 1/4-inch thickness.

4. Use cookie cutters to cut out shapes and place them on the prepared baking mat.

5. Bake for 25-30 minutes until biscuits are firm and lightly browned.

6. Allow to cool completely before serving.

Nutritional Information: Each biscuit provides approximately 70 calories, 3g protein, 3g fat, 8g carbohydrates, 1g Fiber

Spinach and Cheese Biscuits

Cooking Time: 20-25 minutes

Servings: Makes about 20 biscuits

Ingredients:

- 1 cup chopped spinach, cooked and drained

- 1/2 cup shredded cheese (cheddar or mozzarella)

- 2 cups oat flour

- 1 egg

Instructions:

1. Preheat your oven to 350°F (175°C) and line a baking sheet with a silicone baking mat.

2. In a mixing bowl, combine chopped cooked spinach, shredded cheese, oat flour, and egg until well combined.

3. Roll out the dough on a floured surface to about 1/4-inch thickness.

4. Use cookie cutters to cut out shapes and place them on the prepared baking mat.

5. Bake for 20-25 minutes until biscuits are firm and lightly browned.

6. Allow to cool completely before serving.

Nutritional Information: Each biscuit provides approximately 55 calories, 2g protein, 2g fat, 7g carbohydrates, 1g Fiber

Turkey and Cranberry Chews

Cooking Time: 3-4 hours

Servings: Makes about 12 chews

Ingredients:

- 1 cup cooked and shredded turkey

- 1/4 cup dried cranberries, chopped

- 2 cups oat flour

- 1 egg

Instructions:

1. Preheat your oven to 250°F (120°C) and line a baking sheet with a silicone baking mat.

2. In a mixing bowl, combine shredded turkey, chopped dried cranberries, oat flour, and egg until well combined.

3. Roll out the dough on a floured surface to about 1/4-inch thickness.

4. Use a knife or pizza cutter to cut the dough into strips.

5. Place the strips on the prepared baking mat.

6. Bake for 3-4 hours until chews are dried and firm.

7. Allow to cool completely before serving.

Nutritional Information: Each chew provides approximately 60 calories, 3g protein, 1.5g fat, 9g carbohydrates, 1g Fiber

Apple and Cheddar Biscuits

Cooking Time: 20-25 minutes

Servings: Makes about 24 biscuits

Ingredients:

- 1 cup grated apple

- 1/2 cup shredded cheddar cheese

- 2 cups oat flour

- 1 egg

Instructions:

1. Preheat your oven to 350°F (175°C) and line a baking sheet with a silicone baking mat.

2. In a mixing bowl, combine grated apple, shredded cheddar cheese, oat flour, and egg until well combined.

3. Roll out the dough on a floured surface to about 1/4-inch thickness.

4. Use cookie cutters to cut out shapes and place them on the prepared baking mat.

5. Bake for 20-25 minutes until biscuits are firm and lightly browned.

6. Allow to cool completely before serving.

Nutritional Information: Each biscuit provides approximately 50 calories, 2g protein, 2g fat, 7g carbohydrates, 1g Fiber

Bacon and Peanut Butter Bones

Cooking Time: 25-30 minutes

Servings: Makes about 16 bones

Ingredients:

- 1/2 cup cooked and crumbled bacon

- 1/4 cup natural peanut butter

- 2 cups whole wheat flour

- 1 egg

Instructions:

1. Preheat your oven to 350°F (175°C) and line a baking sheet with a silicone baking mat.

2. In a mixing bowl, combine crumbled bacon, peanut butter, whole wheat flour, and egg until a dough forms.

3. Roll out the dough on a floured surface to about 1/4-inch thickness.

4. Use bone-shaped cookie cutters to cut out shapes and place them on the prepared baking mat.

5. Bake for 25-30 minutes until bones are firm and lightly browned.

6. Allow to cool completely before serving.

Nutritional Information: Each bone provides approximately 75 calories, 3g protein, 3.5g fat, 8g carbohydrates, 1g Fiber

Chapter 5

Dog-Nuts, Pup pies and Pup-Tarts

Peanut Butter Dog-Nuts

Cooking Time: 15-20 minutes

Servings: Makes about 12 Dog-Nuts

Ingredients:

- 1 cup whole wheat flour
- 1/4 cup natural peanut butter
- 1/4 cup unsweetened applesauce
- 1 teaspoon baking powder
- 1 egg

Instructions:

1. Preheat your oven to 350°F (175°C) and line a baking sheet with a silicone baking mat.
2. In a mixing bowl, combine whole wheat flour, peanut butter, applesauce, baking powder, and egg until well combined.
3. Transfer the dough to a lightly floured surface and roll out to about 1/4-inch thickness.
4. Use a doughnut cutter or a small round cutter to cut out doughnut shapes.
5. Place the doughnuts on the prepared baking mat.
6. Bake for 15-20 minutes until golden brown and cooked through.
7. Allow to cool completely before serving.

Nutritional Information: Each Dog-Nut provides approximately 70 calories, 2g protein, 3g fat, 8g carbohydrates, 1g Fiber

Pumpkin Pup Pies

Cooking Time: 25-30 minutes

Servings: Makes about 6 Pup Pies

Ingredients:

- 1 cup canned pumpkin puree

- 1/2 cup plain Greek yogurt

- 1/4 cup honey

- 1/2 cup oat flour

- 1 egg

Instructions:

1. Preheat your oven to 350°F (175°C) and line a muffin tin with silicone baking cups.

2. In a mixing bowl, combine pumpkin puree, Greek yogurt, honey, oat flour, and egg until smooth.

3. Spoon the mixture evenly into the muffin cups, filling each about three-quarters full.

4. Bake for 25-30 minutes until set and lightly golden.

5. Allow to cool completely before serving.

Nutritional Information: Each Pup Pie provides approximately 90 calories, 3g protein, 2.5g fat, 15g carbohydrates, 2g Fiber

Blueberry Pup-Tarts

Cooking Time: 20-25 minutes

Servings: Makes about 8 Pup-Tarts

Ingredients:

- 1 cup blueberries, fresh or frozen

- 1/2 cup unsweetened applesauce

- 1 tablespoon honey

- 1 cup oat flour

- 1 egg

Instructions:

1. Preheat your oven to 350°F (175°C) and line a baking sheet with a silicone baking mat.

2. In a small saucepan, heat the blueberries, applesauce, and honey over medium heat until the mixture starts to bubble. Reduce heat and simmer for 5 minutes, then remove from heat and let cool.

3. In a mixing bowl, combine oat flour and egg, then add the cooled blueberry mixture. Mix until well combined.

4. Roll out the dough on a lightly floured surface to about 1/4-inch thickness.

5. Use a square cookie cutter or a knife to cut out tart shapes. Place them on the prepared baking mat.

6. Bake for 20-25 minutes until lightly golden and firm.

7. Allow to cool completely before serving.

Nutritional Information: Each Pup-Tart provides approximately 60 calories, 2g protein, 1.5g fat, 10g carbohydrates, 1g Fiber

Banana and Peanut Butter Dog-Nuts

Cooking Time: 15-20 minutes

Servings: Makes about 12 Dog-Nuts

Ingredients:

- 1 ripe banana, mashed

- 1/4 cup natural peanut butter

- 1/4 cup unsweetened applesauce

- 1 cup whole wheat flour

- 1 teaspoon baking powder

Instructions:

1. Preheat your oven to 350°F (175°C) and line a baking sheet with a silicone baking mat.

2. In a mixing bowl, combine mashed banana, peanut butter, applesauce, whole wheat flour, and baking powder until well combined.

3. Transfer the dough to a lightly floured surface and roll out to about 1/4-inch thickness.

4. Use a doughnut cutter or a small round cutter to cut out doughnut shapes.

5. Place the doughnuts on the prepared baking mat.

6. Bake for 15-20 minutes until golden brown and cooked through.

7. Allow to cool completely before serving.

Nutritional Information: Each Dog-Nut provides approximately 70 calories, 2g protein, 3g fat, 9g carbohydrates, 1g Fiber

Apple Pup Pies

Cooking Time: 25-30 minutes

Servings: Makes about 6 Pup Pies

Ingredients:

- 1 cup grated apple

- 1/4 cup unsweetened applesauce

- 1/4 cup honey

- 1 cup oat flour

- 1 egg

Instructions:

1. Preheat your oven to 350°F (175°C) and line a muffin tin with silicone baking cups.

2. In a mixing bowl, combine grated apple, applesauce, honey, oat flour, and egg until well mixed.

3. Spoon the mixture evenly into the muffin cups, filling each about three-quarters full.

4. Bake for 25-30 minutes until set and lightly golden.

5. Allow to cool completely before serving.

Nutritional Information: Each Pup Pie provides approximately 90 calories, 2g protein, 2.5g fat, 15g carbohydrates, 2g Fiber

Strawberry Pup-Tarts

Cooking Time: 20-25 minutes

Servings: Makes about 8 Pup-Tarts

Ingredients:

- 1 cup chopped strawberries
- 1/2 cup unsweetened applesauce
- 1 tablespoon honey
- 1 cup oat flour
- 1 egg

Instructions:

1. Preheat your oven to 350°F (175°C) and line a baking sheet with a silicone baking mat.

2. In a small saucepan, heat the strawberries, applesauce, and honey over medium heat until the mixture starts to bubble. Reduce heat and simmer for 5 minutes, then remove from heat and let cool.

3. In a mixing bowl, combine oat flour and egg, then add the cooled strawberry mixture. Mix until well combined.

4. Roll out the dough on a lightly floured surface to about 1/4-inch thickness.

5. Use a square cookie cutter or a knife to cut out tart shapes. Place them on the prepared baking mat.

6. Bake for 20-25 minutes until lightly golden and firm.

7. Allow to cool completely before serving.

Nutritional Information: Each Pup-Tart provides approximately 60 calories, 2g protein, 1.5g fat, 10g carbohydrates, 1g Fiber

Carrot and Cheese Dog-Nuts

Cooking Time: 15-20 minutes

Servings: Makes about 12 Dog-Nuts

Ingredients:

- 1 cup grated carrot

- 1/4 cup shredded cheese (cheddar or mozzarella)

- 1/4 cup unsweetened applesauce

- 1 cup oat flour

- 1 egg

Instructions:

1. Preheat your oven to 350°F (175°C) and line a baking sheet with a silicone baking mat.

2. In a mixing bowl, combine grated carrot, shredded cheese, applesauce, oat flour, and egg until well combined.

3. Transfer the dough to a lightly floured surface and roll out to about 1/4-inch thickness.

4. Use a doughnut cutter or a small round cutter to cut out doughnut shapes.

5. Place the doughnuts on the prepared baking mat.

6. Bake for 15-20 minutes until golden brown and cooked through.

7. Allow to cool completely before serving.

Nutritional Information: Each Dog-Nut provides approximately 70 calories, 2.5g protein, 3g fat, 9g carbohydrates, 1g Fiber

Chicken and Vegetable Pup Pies

Cooking Time: 25-30 minutes

Servings: Makes about 6 Pup Pies

Ingredients:

- 1 cup cooked and shredded chicken

- 1/2 cup finely chopped mixed vegetables (carrots, peas, green beans)

- 1/4 cup unsweetened chicken broth

- 1/2 cup oat flour

- 1 egg

Instructions:

1. Preheat your oven to 350°F (175°C) and line a muffin tin with silicone baking cups.

2. In a mixing bowl, combine shredded chicken, chopped vegetables, chicken broth, oat flour, and egg until well mixed.

3. Spoon the mixture evenly into the muffin cups, filling each about three-quarters full.

4. Bake for 25-30 minutes until set and lightly golden.

5. Allow to cool completely before serving.

Nutritional Information: Each Pup Pie provides approximately 100 calories, 5g protein, 2.5g fat, 12g carbohydrates, 2g Fiber

Spinach and Bacon Pup-Tarts

Cooking Time: 20-25 minutes

Servings: Makes about 8 Pup-Tarts

Ingredients:

- 1 cup chopped spinach, cooked and drained

- 1/4 cup cooked and crumbled bacon

- 1/4 cup unsweetened applesauce

- 1 cup oat flour

- 1 egg

Instructions:

1. Preheat your oven to 350°F (175°C) and line a baking sheet with a silicone baking mat.

2. In a mixing bowl, combine chopped spinach, crumbled bacon, applesauce, oat flour, and egg until well combined.

3. Roll out the dough on a lightly floured surface to about 1/4-inch thickness.

4. Use a square cookie cutter or a knife to cut out tart shapes. Place them on the prepared baking mat.

5. Bake for 20-25 minutes until lightly golden and firm.

6. Allow to cool completely before serving.

Nutritional Information: Each Pup-Tart provides approximately 80 calories, 3g protein, 2.5g fat, 10g carbohydrates, 1g Fiber

Beef and Potato Dog-Nuts

Cooking Time: 15-20 minutes

Servings: Makes about 12 Dog-Nuts

Ingredients:

- 1/2 cup cooked and mashed potato

- 1/2 cup cooked and shredded beef

- 1/4 cup unsweetened applesauce

- 1 cup oat flour

- 1 egg

Instructions:

1. Preheat your oven to 350°F (175°C) and line a baking sheet with a silicone baking mat.

2. In a mixing bowl, combine mashed potato, shredded beef, applesauce, oat flour, and egg until well combined.

3. Transfer the dough to a lightly floured surface and roll out to about 1/4-inch thickness.

4. Use a doughnut cutter or a small round cutter to cut out doughnut shapes.

5. Place the doughnuts on the prepared baking mat.

6. Bake for 15-20 minutes until golden brown and cooked through.

7. Allow to cool completely before serving.

Nutritional Information: Each Dog-Nut provides approximately 80 calories, 3g protein, 2.5g fat, 10g carbohydrates, 1g Fiber

Chapter 6
Gluten-free options

Sweet Potato and Peanut Butter Treats

Cooking Time: 25-30 minutes

Servings: Makes about 20 treats

Ingredients:

- 1 cup cooked and mashed sweet potato
- 1/4 cup natural peanut butter
- 2 cups oat flour
- 1 egg

Instructions:

1. Preheat your oven to 350°F (175°C) and line a baking sheet with a silicone baking mat.

2. In a mixing bowl, combine mashed sweet potato, peanut butter, oat flour, and egg until well combined.

3. Roll out the dough on a floured surface to about 1/4-inch thickness.

4. Use cookie cutters to cut out shapes and place them on the prepared baking mat.

5. Bake for 25-30 minutes until treats are firm and lightly browned.

6. Allow to cool completely before serving.

Nutritional Information: Each treat provides approximately 45 calories, 2g protein, 2g fat, 6g carbohydrates, 1g Fiber

Banana and Blueberry Biscuits

Cooking Time: 20-25 minutes

Servings: Makes about 18 biscuits

Ingredients:

- 1 ripe banana, mashed

- 1/2 cup blueberries, mashed

- 2 cups oat flour

- 1 egg

Instructions:

1. Preheat your oven to 350°F (175°C) and line a baking sheet with a silicone baking mat.

2. In a mixing bowl, combine mashed banana, mashed blueberries, oat flour, and egg until well combined.

3. Roll out the dough on a floured surface to about 1/4-inch thickness.

4. Use cookie cutters to cut out shapes and place them on the prepared baking mat.

5. Bake for 20-25 minutes until biscuits are firm and lightly browned.

6. Allow to cool completely before serving.

Nutritional Information: Each biscuit provides approximately 40 calories, 1.5g protein, 1g fat, 7g carbohydrates, 1g Fiber

Pumpkin and Cranberry Cookies

Cooking Time: 15-18 minutes

Servings: Makes about 24 cookies

Ingredients:

- 1 cup canned pumpkin puree

- 1/4 cup dried cranberries, chopped

- 2 cups oat flour

- 1 egg

Instructions:

1. Preheat your oven to 350°F (175°C) and line a baking sheet with a silicone baking mat.

2. In a mixing bowl, combine pumpkin puree, chopped dried cranberries, oat flour, and egg until a dough forms.

3. Roll out the dough on a floured surface to about 1/4-inch thickness.

4. Use cookie cutters to cut out shapes and place them on the prepared baking mat.

5. Bake for 15-18 minutes until cookies are firm and lightly browned.

6. Allow to cool completely before storing in an airtight container.

Nutritional Information: Each cookie provides approximately 35 calories, 1g protein, 1g fat, 6g carbohydrates, 1g Fiber

Carrot and Cheese Biscuits

Cooking Time: 20-25 minutes

Servings: Makes about 20 biscuits

Ingredients:

- 1 cup grated carrot

- 1/2 cup shredded cheese (cheddar or mozzarella)

- 2 cups oat flour

- 1 egg

Instructions:

1. Preheat your oven to 350°F (175°C) and line a baking sheet with a silicone baking mat.

2. In a mixing bowl, combine grated carrot, shredded cheese, oat flour, and egg until well combined.

3. Roll out the dough on a floured surface to about 1/4-inch thickness.

4. Use cookie cutters to cut out shapes and place them on the prepared baking mat.

5. Bake for 20-25 minutes until biscuits are firm and lightly browned.

6. Allow to cool completely before serving.

Nutritional Information: Each biscuit provides approximately 50 calories, 2g protein, 2g fat, 7g carbohydrates, 1g Fiber

Apple and Cinnamon Bites

Cooking Time: 15-18 minutes

Servings: Makes about 24 bites

Ingredients:

- 1 cup grated apple

- 1 teaspoon ground cinnamon

- 2 cups oat flour

- 1 egg

Instructions:

1. Preheat your oven to 350°F (175°C) and line a baking sheet with a silicone baking mat.

2. In a mixing bowl, combine grated apple, ground cinnamon, oat flour, and egg until well combined.

3. Roll the dough into small balls and place them on the prepared baking mat.

4. Flatten each ball slightly with your fingers.

5. Bake for 15-18 minutes until bites are firm and lightly browned.

6. Allow to cool completely before serving.

Nutritional Information: Each bite provides approximately 30 calories, 1g protein, 1g fat, 5g carbohydrates, 1g Fiber

Spinach and Chicken Balls

Cooking Time: 12-15 minutes

Servings: Makes about 18 balls

Ingredients:

- 1 cup chopped spinach, cooked and drained

- 1/2 cup cooked and shredded chicken

- 2 cups oat flour

- 1 egg

Instructions:

1. Preheat your oven to 350°F (175°C) and line a baking sheet with a silicone baking mat.

2. In a mixing bowl, combine chopped cooked spinach, shredded chicken, oat flour, and egg until well combined.

3. Roll the mixture into small balls and place them on the prepared baking mat.

4. Flatten each ball slightly with your fingers.

5. Bake for 12-15 minutes until treats are cooked through and lightly golden.

6. Allow to cool completely before serving.

Nutritional Information: Each ball provides approximately 45 calories, 2g protein, 1.5g fat, 6g carbohydrates, 1g Fiber

Pumpkin and Turkey Jerky

Cooking Time: 2-3 hours

Servings: Makes about 12 strips

Ingredients:

- 1 cup canned pumpkin puree

- 1 cup cooked and shredded turkey

- 1 1/2 cups oat flour

Instructions:

1. Preheat your oven to 200°F (95°C) and line a baking sheet with a silicone baking mat.

2. In a mixing bowl, combine pumpkin puree, shredded turkey, and oat flour until a dough forms.

3. Roll out the dough on a floured surface to about 1/8-inch thickness.

4. Cut the dough into strips and place them on the prepared baking mat.

5. Bake for 2-3 hours until the jerky is dried and firm.

6. Allow to cool completely before serving.

Nutritional Information: Each strip provides approximately 40 calories, 2g protein, 1g fat, 5g carbohydrates, 1g Fiber

Coconut and Banana Cookies

Cooking Time: 20-25 minutes

Servings: Makes about 24 cookies

Ingredients:

- 1 ripe banana, mashed

- 1/4 cup coconut flour

- 1/4 cup unsweetened shredded coconut

- 1 egg

Instructions:

1. Preheat your oven to 350°F (175°C) and line a baking sheet with a silicone baking mat.

2. In a mixing bowl, combine mashed banana, coconut flour, shredded coconut, and egg until a dough forms.

3. Drop spoonfuls of the dough onto the prepared baking mat.

4. Flatten each cookie slightly with your fingers.

5. Bake for 20-25 minutes until cookies are firm and lightly browned.

6. Allow to cool completely before serving.

Nutritional Information: Each cookie provides approximately 25 calories, 1g protein, 1g fat, 4g carbohydrates, 1g Fiber

Carrot and Zucchini Biscuits

Cooking Time: 20-25 minutes

Servings: Makes about 20 biscuits

Ingredients:

- 1 cup grated carrot

- 1 cup grated zucchini

- 2 cups oat flour

- 1 egg

Instructions:

1. Preheat your oven to 350°F (175°C) and line a baking sheet with a silicone baking mat.

2. In a mixing bowl, combine grated carrot, grated zucchini, oat flour, and egg until well combined.

3. Roll out the dough on a floured surface to about 1/4-inch thickness.

4. Use cookie cutters to cut out shapes and place them on the prepared baking mat.

5. Bake for 20-25 minutes until biscuits are firm and lightly browned.

6. Allow to cool completely before serving.

Nutritional Information: Each biscuit provides approximately 45 calories, 1.5g protein, 1g fat, 7g carbohydrates, 1g Fiber

Apple and Pumpkin Bites

Cooking Time: 15-18 minutes

Servings: Makes about 24 bites

Ingredients:

- 1 cup grated apple

- 1/2 cup canned pumpkin puree

- 2 cups oat flour

- 1 egg

Instructions:

1. Preheat your oven to 350°F (175°C) and line a baking sheet with a silicone baking mat.

2. In a mixing bowl, combine grated apple, pumpkin puree, oat flour, and egg until well combined.

3. Roll the dough into small balls and place them on the prepared baking mat.

4. Flatten each ball slightly with your fingers.

5. Bake for 15-18 minutes until bites are firm and lightly browned.

6. Allow to cool completely before serving.

Nutritional Information: Each bite provides approximately 35 calories, 1g protein, 1g fat, 6g carbohydrates, 1g Fiber

CONCLUSION

As we draw near to the end of this culinary odyssey through the world of homemade dog treats, I am overwhelmed with gratitude for the privilege of sharing this journey with you. Together, we have traversed the colorful landscapes of flavor and nutrition, exploring the boundless possibilities of nourishing our beloved canine companions with wholesome, homemade delights.

Throughout the pages of this cookbook, we have not only discovered tantalizing recipes but also forged a deeper connection with the furry friends who grace our lives with their unconditional love and unwavering loyalty. From the first tentative steps in the kitchen to the triumphant creation of delectable treats, each moment has been infused with a sense of joy, creativity, and purpose.

But as we bid farewell to the recipes and stories that have enriched our lives, I am reminded that our journey does not end here. In fact, it is just beginning. As you bring these recipes into your own kitchen and share them with your cherished companions, I encourage you to embark on your own culinary adventures.

Experiment with new ingredients, tweak the recipes to suit your dog's preferences, and let your imagination soar as you create culinary masterpieces that will delight and nourish your furry friends. And as you immerse yourself in the art of cooking for dogs, I invite you to embrace the spirit of exploration and discovery that has guided us thus far.

But beyond the realm of the kitchen, I encourage you to reflect on the deeper significance of our journey. For in the act of nourishing our dogs with homemade treats, we are not merely satisfying their physical hunger; we are also nurturing their souls and strengthening the bond that unites us as companions on life's journey.

In the gentle wag of a tail, the eager anticipation of a treat, and the loving gaze of a devoted friend, we find echoes of our own humanity and reminders of the profound connection that exists between humans and dogs. And as we honor this connection through the act of cooking and sharing, we affirm the beauty of life and the joy of companionship.

As we part ways, I invite you to share your thoughts, experiences, and feedback with me. Your insights and honest reviews are invaluable to me as I continue to refine and improve my craft. Whether you have a suggestion for a new recipe, a question about a particular ingredient, or simply want to share the joy of cooking for your canine companion, I am here to listen and learn.

Together, let us continue to celebrate the bond between humans and dogs, one delicious treat at a time. Thank you for joining me on this culinary adventure, and may your kitchen always be filled with the laughter, love, and warmth of your faithful companions.

Bonus 1
Breed-Specific Care Tips

Understanding the unique characteristics and needs of different dog breeds is essential for providing optimal care and ensuring the well-being of your canine companion. In this chapter, we'll explore breed-specific care tips tailored to various breeds, covering topics such as grooming, exercise requirements, health considerations, and common behavioral traits.

Small Breeds

Small dog breeds, such as Chihuahuas, Pomeranians, and Yorkshire Terriers, often have special care requirements due to their petite size and delicate frames.

Grooming: Small breeds typically have long, silky coats that require regular grooming to prevent mats and tangles. Daily brushing and occasional baths are recommended to keep their coats healthy and shiny.

Exercise: Despite their small size, many small breeds have high energy levels and enjoy regular walks and play sessions. However, it's essential to be mindful of their limitations and avoid strenuous activities that could cause injury.

Health Considerations: Small breeds are prone to dental issues, such as tartar buildup and tooth decay, so regular dental care, including brushing and dental chews, is important. Additionally, they may be susceptible to hypoglycaemia, so it's crucial to monitor their diet and provide frequent, small meals throughout the day.

Behavioural Traits: Small breeds are often known for their bold personalities and tendency to be protective of their owners. Socialization from an early age can help prevent behavioural problems, such as excessive barking or aggression towards strangers.

Large Breeds

Large dog breeds, such as Labrador Retrievers, German Shepherds, and Golden Retrievers, require special care due to their size, strength, and specific health considerations.

Grooming: Large breeds often have double coats that shed seasonally, so regular brushing is necessary to remove loose fur and minimize shedding. Additionally, regular nail trimming and ear cleaning are essential parts of their grooming routine.

Exercise: Large breeds have higher exercise requirements and benefit from daily walks, vigorous play sessions, and activities that engage their minds and bodies. Adequate exercise helps prevent obesity and promotes overall health and well-being.

Health Considerations: Large breeds are prone to orthopaedic issues, such as hip dysplasia and arthritis, so it's crucial to provide proper nutrition, maintain a healthy weight, and avoid activities that strain their joints, especially during puppyhood. Regular veterinary check-ups and preventive care are also important for early detection and management of potential health problems.

Behavioural Traits: Large breeds are often gentle giants known for their loyalty, intelligence, and gentle demeanour. However, they may require consistent training and socialization to prevent behavioural problems, such as leash pulling or jumping on people.

Toy Breeds

Toy dog breeds, such as Maltese, Shih Tzus, and Toy Poodles, have their own set of care requirements due to their small size and delicate features.

Grooming: Toy breeds often have long, flowing coats that require regular grooming to prevent mats and tangles. Gentle brushing and frequent baths are necessary to maintain their coat health and cleanliness.

Exercise: Despite their diminutive size, toy breeds still need regular exercise to stay healthy and active. Short walks, indoor play sessions, and interactive toys are ideal for meeting their exercise needs without overexertion.

Health Considerations: Toy breeds are prone to dental issues, respiratory problems, and luxating patellas, so regular dental care, monitoring for signs of respiratory distress, and avoiding activities that put strain on their joints are important aspects of their care.

Behavioral Traits: Toy breeds are often affectionate, lively, and sociable companions. However, they may be prone to separation anxiety and may require extra attention and companionship to prevent boredom and stress-related behaviors.

Understanding the specific needs and characteristics of different dog breeds is crucial for providing appropriate care and ensuring the well-being of your furry friend. By tailoring your care routine to meet the unique requirements of your dog's breed, you can help them lead a happy, healthy, and fulfilling life.

In this Bonus chapter, we covered care tips for small breeds, large breeds, and toy breeds, highlighting their unique grooming needs, exercise requirements, health considerations, and behavioral traits. By applying these breed-specific care tips, you can ensure that your dog receives the best possible care tailored to their individual needs and characteristics.

Bonus 2

30 DAY MEAL PLAN

Day	Breakfast	Lunch	Dinner	Treats
1	Scrambled eggs with spinach	Grilled chicken breast with carrots	Turkey and sweet potato stew	Frozen banana slices
2	Oatmeal with blueberries	Salmon and brown rice	Beef and vegetable stir-fry	Carrot sticks with peanut butter
3	Greek yogurt with strawberries	Tuna salad with green beans	Quinoa and turkey meatballs	Frozen pumpkin cubes
4	Cottage cheese with apple slices	Turkey and vegetable soup	Baked sweet potato with chicken	Apple slices with cheese
5	Mashed banana with peanut butter	Beef and barley stew	Fish and sweet potato mash	Frozen watermelon cubes
6	Pumpkin puree with cinnamon	Chicken and quinoa salad	Lamb and brown rice casserole	Green bean crunchies
7	Scrambled eggs with cheese	Turkey and cranberry sandwich	Pork and vegetable kebabs	Frozen blueberry yogurt drops

8	Greek yogurt with honey	Beef and vegetable stir-fry	Salmon and sweet potato patties	Carrot and apple muffins
9	Cottage cheese with pineapple	Tuna and chickpea salad	Chicken and rice pilaf	Frozen strawberry slices
10	Mashed banana with coconut flakes	Beef and pumpkin curry	Turkey and quinoa stuffed peppers	Green bean and carrot chips
11	Pumpkin puree with almond butter	Lamb and barley soup	Fish and vegetable stir-fry	Frozen peach slices
12	Scrambled eggs with zucchini	Chicken and sweet potato stew	Beef and brown rice casserole	Frozen pineapple chunks
13	Greek yogurt with mixed berries	Turkey and spinach wrap	Salmon and quinoa bowl	Frozen mango cubes
14	Cottage cheese with strawberries	Beef and vegetable stir-fry	Chicken and lentil curry	Frozen raspberry yogurt drops
15	Mashed banana with blueberries	Pork and apple salad	Turkey and barley pilaf	Carrot and pumpkin biscuits
16	Pumpkin puree with peanut butter	Fish and quinoa salad	Beef and sweet potato hash	Frozen kiwi slices

17	Scrambled eggs with carrots	Chicken and brown rice	Salmon and vegetable stir-fry	Frozen blackberry yogurt drops
18	Greek yogurt with banana	Beef and sweet potato stew	Lamb and barley risotto	Green bean and apple crunchies
19	Cottage cheese with mango	Turkey and cranberry quinoa	Pork and vegetable stir-fry	Frozen apricot slices
20	Mashed banana with pumpkin seeds	Chicken and barley soup	Fish and vegetable curry	Frozen pear slices
21	Pumpkin puree with honey	Beef and spinach wrap	Turkey and quinoa salad	Carrot and banana muffins
22	Scrambled eggs with broccoli	Pork and sweet potato stew	Salmon and brown rice pilaf	Frozen cherry tomatoes
23	Greek yogurt with peach	Chicken and lentil curry	Beef and vegetable stir-fry	Frozen cranberry yogurt drops
24	Cottage cheese with raspberries	Turkey and pumpkin stew	Lamb and quinoa salad	Green bean and blueberry crunchies
25	Mashed banana with strawberries	Fish and vegetable stir-fry	Pork and barley casserole	Frozen plum slices

26	Pumpkin puree with almond butter	Beef and quinoa salad	Chicken and brown rice pilaf	Frozen grape slices
27	Scrambled eggs with sweet potato	Turkey and spinach curry	Salmon and vegetable stir-fry	Carrot and apple chips
28	Greek yogurt with mixed berries	Chicken and brown rice	Beef and sweet potato stew	Frozen strawberry yogurt drops
29	Cottage cheese with pineapple	Beef and vegetable stir-fry	Lamb and barley soup	Frozen watermelon balls
30	Mashed banana with blueberries	Turkey and quinoa salad	Fish and sweet potato mash	Carrot and pumpkin biscuits

MEAL PLANNER JOURNAL

WEEKLY —

Meal Planner

Week of:

Monday

BREAKFAST

LUNCH

DINNER

SNACK

Tuesday

BREAKFAST

LUNCH

DINNER

SNACK

Wednesday

BREAKFAST

LUNCH

DINNER

SNACK

Thursday

BREAKFAST

LUNCH

DINNER

SNACK

Friday

BREAKFAST

LUNCH

DINNER

SNACK

Saturday

BREAKFAST

LUNCH

DINNER

SNACK

Sunday

BREAKFAST

LUNCH

DINNER

SNACK

NOTES:

Meal Planner

Week of:

Monday			Tuesday			Wednesday	

Monday

BREAKFAST

LUNCH

DINNER

SNACK

Tuesday

BREAKFAST

LUNCH

DINNER

SNACK

Wednesday

BREAKFAST

LUNCH

DINNER

SNACK

Thursday

BREAKFAST

LUNCH

DINNER

SNACK

Friday

BREAKFAST

LUNCH

DINNER

SNACK

Saturday

BREAKFAST

LUNCH

DINNER

SNACK

Sunday

BREAKFAST

LUNCH

DINNER

SNACK

NOTES:

Meal Planner

Week of:

Monday		
BREAKFAST		
LUNCH		
DINNER		
SNACK		

Tuesday		
BREAKFAST		
LUNCH		
DINNER		
SNACK		

Wednesday		
BREAKFAST		
LUNCH		
DINNER		
SNACK		

Thursday		
BREAKFAST		
LUNCH		
DINNER		
SNACK		

Friday		
BREAKFAST		
LUNCH		
DINNER		
SNACK		

Saturday		
BREAKFAST		
LUNCH		
DINNER		
SNACK		

Sunday		
BREAKFAST		
LUNCH		
DINNER		
SNACK		

NOTES:

WEEKLY —

Meal Planner

Week of:

Monday	Tuesday	Wednesday
BREAKFAST	BREAKFAST	BREAKFAST
LUNCH	LUNCH	LUNCH
DINNER	DINNER	DINNER
SNACK	SNACK	SNACK

Thursday	Friday	Saturday
BREAKFAST	BREAKFAST	BREAKFAST
LUNCH	LUNCH	LUNCH
DINNER	DINNER	DINNER
SNACK	SNACK	SNACK

Sunday	NOTES:
BREAKFAST	
LUNCH	
DINNER	
SNACK	

Meal Planner

Week of:

Monday		
BREAKFAST		
LUNCH		
DINNER		
SNACK		

Tuesday		
BREAKFAST		
LUNCH		
DINNER		
SNACK		

Wednesday		
BREAKFAST		
LUNCH		
DINNER		
SNACK		

Thursday		
BREAKFAST		
LUNCH		
DINNER		
SNACK		

Friday		
BREAKFAST		
LUNCH		
DINNER		
SNACK		

Saturday		
BREAKFAST		
LUNCH		
DINNER		
SNACK		

Sunday		
BREAKFAST		
LUNCH		
DINNER		
SNACK		

NOTES:

WEEKLY —

Meal Planner

Week of:

Monday	Tuesday	Wednesday
BREAKFAST	BREAKFAST	BREAKFAST
LUNCH	LUNCH	LUNCH
DINNER	DINNER	DINNER
SNACK	SNACK	SNACK

Thursday	Friday	Saturday
BREAKFAST	BREAKFAST	BREAKFAST
LUNCH	LUNCH	LUNCH
DINNER	DINNER	DINNER
SNACK	SNACK	SNACK

Sunday	NOTES:
BREAKFAST	
LUNCH	
DINNER	
SNACK	

WEEKLY —

Meal Planner

Week of:

Monday

BREAKFAST

LUNCH

DINNER

SNACK

Tuesday

BREAKFAST

LUNCH

DINNER

SNACK

Wednesday

BREAKFAST

LUNCH

DINNER

SNACK

Thursday

BREAKFAST

LUNCH

DINNER

SNACK

Friday

BREAKFAST

LUNCH

DINNER

SNACK

Saturday

BREAKFAST

LUNCH

DINNER

SNACK

Sunday

BREAKFAST

LUNCH

DINNER

SNACK

NOTES:

WEEKLY —

Meil Planner

Week of:

Monday	Tuesday	Wednesday
BREAKFAST	BREAKFAST	BREAKFAST
LUNCH	LUNCH	LUNCH
DINNER	DINNER	DINNER
SNACK	SNACK	SNACK

Thursday	Friday	Saturday
BREAKFAST	BREAKFAST	BREAKFAST
LUNCH	LUNCH	LUNCH
DINNER	DINNER	DINNER
SNACK	SNACK	SNACK

Sunday	NOTES:
BREAKFAST	
LUNCH	
DINNER	
SNACK	

Meal Planner

Week of:

Monday

BREAKFAST

LUNCH

DINNER

SNACK

Tuesday

BREAKFAST

LUNCH

DINNER

SNACK

Wednesday

BREAKFAST

LUNCH

DINNER

SNACK

Thursday

BREAKFAST

LUNCH

DINNER

SNACK

Friday

BREAKFAST

LUNCH

DINNER

SNACK

Saturday

BREAKFAST

LUNCH

DINNER

SNACK

Sunday

BREAKFAST

LUNCH

DINNER

SNACK

NOTES:

Meal Planner

Week of:

Monday		Tuesday		Wednesday
BREAKFAST		BREAKFAST		BREAKFAST
LUNCH		LUNCH		LUNCH
DINNER		DINNER		DINNER
SNACK		SNACK		SNACK

Thursday		Friday		Saturday
BREAKFAST		BREAKFAST		BREAKFAST
LUNCH		LUNCH		LUNCH
DINNER		DINNER		DINNER
SNACK		SNACK		SNACK

Sunday		NOTES:
BREAKFAST		
LUNCH		
DINNER		
SNACK		

MONTHLY —

Meal Planner

Month of:

Sun	Mon	Tues	Wed	Thurs	Fri	Sai

Made in United States
Orlando, FL
05 June 2025

61879645R00044